EASY DUMPLINGS COOKBOOK

From Jiaozi To Wontons And Baozi The 25 Chinese Recipes You Really Need To Know

Emma Yang

PREFACE

If you've ever found yourself savoring the sublime simplicity of a perfectly prepared dumpling and wondered if you could recreate that magic in your own kitchen, this cookbook is your golden ticket. We're about to embark on a culinary journey from the bustling markets of Beijing to the serene tearooms of Kyoto and onto the charming streets of Tbilisi—handpicking the most scrumptious dumpling recipes each region has to offer.

Dumplings are the embodiment of comfort food, prevalent in almost every cuisine, yet in none are they so varied, intricate, and delightfully surprising as in Chinese cuisine. In this book, I curated a selection of the most iconic Chinese dumplings—from the world-renowned Jiaozi and Wontons to the savory Baozi. Yet our journey doesn't end there. For the curious and adventurous, I included a sprinkling of delectable dumpling recipes from other regions like Japan and Georgia, offering you a truly global culinary experience.
This cookbook is not just about recipes—it's about equipping you with the skills and knowledge you need to craft these culinary jewels at home.

You'll learn how to mix and knead the dough to the perfect consistency and how to artfully fold your dumplings to give them the classic look we all love. You'll explore fillings that range from traditional to creative, each meticulously chosen to please the palate and suit the dumpling style.

I understand that cookbooks can sometimes be intimidating, filled with unfamiliar terminology and daunting steps. That's why I have designed "Easy Dumplings Cookbook" to be accessible to all. Each recipe is broken down into easy-to-follow steps, accompanied by high-quality, color photos that guide you through each part of the process. You'll find handy tips and tricks sprinkled throughout the pages to assist you in mastering dumpling making. So, whether you're a novice cook or a seasoned chef looking to expand your repertoire, this book has something for you.

"Easy Dumplings Cookbook" celebrates the humble dumpling in all its glory. Beyond the delectable recipes, it also paints a vivid picture of the rich traditions and cultural significance behind these beloved food parcels. It's an invitation to cook and connect with the heart of these culinary traditions, fostering a deeper appreciation for this universally adored food item.

Dumplings are about togetherness, gathering around the table with family or friends, and sharing the joy and warmth that comes from a perfectly cooked, steaming parcel of deliciousness. And that's exactly what this cookbook aims to bring into your home—unforgettable moments, delectable flavors, and the invaluable skill of making dumplings from scratch.

We invite you to roll up your sleeves, dust off your countertop, and embark on this exciting culinary journey. Let's demystify dumplings together and create mouth-watering memories, one delicious bite at a time.

TYPES OF DUMPLINGS

Chinese cuisine is home to a vast array of dumplings, each with its unique characteristics, fillings, and regional variants. Here are some of the most famous Chinese dumplings but remember that each type of dumpling can have many variations, and the fillings can vary based on regional preferences and personal tastes. The same goes for the recipes in this cookbook: feel free to change the ingredients and have fun. Happy cooking!

Jiaozi
Perhaps the most iconic dumpling, Jiaozi are crescent-shaped dumplings often associated with Chinese New Year celebrations. They are typically filled with pork, cabbage, and chives, but there are also many other varieties.

Baozi
These are large, fluffy, steamed buns with a variety of potential fillings, from savory (such as barbecued pork) to sweet (like red bean paste).

Har Gow
A Cantonese specialty, these are delicate, translucent shrimp dumplings typically served in dim sum restaurants

Siu Mai
Another dim sum staple, Siu Mai are open-topped dumplings usually filled with pork, shrimp, and mushrooms.

Zongzi
Though not a dumpling in the traditional sense, these glutinous rice packets wrapped in bamboo leaves and filled with a variety of ingredients (like pork, red bean, or salted egg yolk) are a must-mention. They are traditionally eaten during the Dragon Boat Festival.

Xiaolongbao
These soup dumplings are filled with meat and a flavorful broth. They are often served with vinegar and ginger.

Tangyuan
Sweet dumplings made from glutinous rice flour and filled with a sweet substance like black sesame, red bean paste, or peanut butter. They are usually served in a sweet soup and are traditionally eaten during the Lantern Festival.

Jiaozi

Jiaozi, also known as Chinese dumplings, are a beloved dish in Chinese cuisine, often enjoyed during Chinese New Year celebrations and family gatherings. They are made with a simple dough and filled with a variety of fillings, with ground pork and cabbage being one of the most traditional and popular combinations.

The dumplings are shaped into a half-moon or pleated crescent shape and are usually boiled, but they can also be steamed or pan-fried to create a crisp exterior. A tangy, savory dipping sauce usually accompanies the dumplings, adding an extra layer of flavor.

Creating jiaozi can be a communal and festive activity, with family members often gathering around to help make the dumplings. Eating jiaozi is not only a culinary delight but also a cultural and social experience, bringing people together to enjoy good food and good company.

4 SERVINGS   120 MINUTES   350 KCAL   EASY

INGREDIENTS

For the Dough:
- 2 cups all-purpose flour
- 1/2 to 3/4 cup water

For the Filling:
- 1/2 pound ground pork
- 1 cup finely chopped Napa cabbage
- 2 green onions, finely chopped
- 1 tablespoon soy sauce
- 1 tablespoon Chinese rice wine or dry sherry
- 1 teaspoon sesame oil
- 1/2 teaspoon salt
- 1/4 teaspoon white pepper

For the Dipping Sauce:
- 1/4 cup soy sauce
- 1 tablespoon Chinese black vinegar or balsamic vinegar
- 1/2 teaspoon sesame oil
- 1/2 teaspoon sugar
- Chili oil (optional)

DIRECTIONS

1. **Make the Dough:** In a large mixing bowl, gradually add the water to the flour and knead into a smooth dough. This process should take about 10 minutes. Cover with a damp cloth and let the dough rest for an hour.

2. **Prepare the Filling:** In a large bowl, combine the ground pork, cabbage, green onions, soy sauce, rice wine, sesame oil, salt, and white pepper. Mix well until the ingredients are thoroughly combined.

3. **Assemble the Dumplings:** Divide the rested dough into 40 equal pieces. Roll each piece into a small, round disc about 3 inches in diameter.

4. Place a small spoonful of the filling in the center of each dough circle. Fold the dough over the filling, creating a half-moon shape, and press the edges to seal. Make sure there are no air pockets. Repeat with the rest of the dough and filling.

5. **Cook the Dumplings:** Bring a large pot of water to a boil. Add half of the dumplings, giving them a gentle stir so they don't stick together. Bring the water back to a boil, and add 1/2 cup of cold water. Cover and repeat. When the dumplings come to a boil for a third time, they are ready. Use a slotted spoon to remove the dumplings from the pot and drain well.

6. **Make the Dipping Sauce:** Combine the soy sauce, vinegar, sesame oil, sugar, and chili oil (if using) in a small bowl. Stir until the sugar is dissolved.

7. **Serve:** Serve the dumplings hot with the dipping sauce.

Cooking tips:
- You can also pan-fry the dumplings to make potstickers: heat a small amount of oil in a nonstick pan, add the dumplings, and cook until browned on the bottom. Then, add a few tablespoons of water and cover the pan. Steam until the dumplings are cooked through and the water has evaporated.

1,800 YEARS OLD

Chinese dumplings, known as jiaozi, have a rich history spanning over 1,800 years and are considered a traditional Chinese dish.

Guotie

Guotie, commonly known as potstickers in the West, are a type of Chinese dumpling that's pan-fried to achieve a crispy bottom. The name guotie literally translates to "pot stick," referring to how the dumplings stick to the pan and get a crispy bottom during cooking.

Guotie are typically made with a filling of ground pork, cabbage, and other ingredients like chives and shiitake mushrooms, all wrapped in a simple dough. The dumplings are first pan-fried on one side, then water is added and the pan is covered to steam and cook the dumplings through. The result is a dumpling that's crispy on the bottom, tender on the top, and juicy on the inside. Served with a tangy dipping sauce, guotie are a delightful mix of textures and flavors that make them a popular dish in Chinese cuisine.

 4 SERVINGS    90 MINUTES   400 KCAL   EASY

INGREDIENTS

For the Dough:
- 2 cups all-purpose flour
- 1/2 to 3/4 cup water

For the Filling:
- 1/2 pound ground pork
- 1/2 cup finely chopped Napa cabbage
- 1/4 cup finely chopped chives
- 1/2 cup finely chopped shiitake mushrooms
- 1 tablespoon soy sauce
- 1 tablespoon Chinese rice wine or dry sherry
- 1 teaspoon sesame oil
- 1/2 teaspoon salt
- 1/4 teaspoon white pepper

For the Dipping Sauce:
- 1/4 cup soy sauce
- 1 tablespoon Chinese black vinegar or balsamic vinegar
- 1/2 teaspoon sesame oil
- 1/2 teaspoon sugar
- Chili oil (optional)

DIRECTIONS

1. **Make the Dough:** In a large mixing bowl, gradually add the water to the flour and knead into a smooth dough. This process should take about 10 minutes. Cover with a damp cloth and let the dough rest for an hour.
2. **Prepare the Filling:** In a large bowl, combine the ground pork, cabbage, chives, shiitake mushrooms, soy sauce, rice wine, sesame oil, salt, and white pepper. Mix well until the ingredients are thoroughly combined.
3. **Assemble the Dumplings:** Divide the rested dough into 40 equal pieces. Roll each piece into a small, round disc about 3 inches in diameter.
4. Place a small spoonful of the filling in the center of each dough circle. Fold the dough over the filling, creating a half-moon shape, and press the edges to seal. Make sure there are no air pockets. Repeat with the rest of the dough and filling.
5. **Cook the Dumplings:** Heat a tablespoon of oil in a large non-stick pan over medium-high heat. Place the dumplings in the pan, flat side down, and cook until the bottoms are golden brown, about 2-3 minutes.
6. Pour 1/4 cup of water into the pan and immediately cover with a lid. Let the dumplings steam for about 5 minutes, until the water has evaporated and the dumplings are cooked through.
7. **Make the Dipping Sauce:** Combine the soy sauce, vinegar, sesame oil, sugar, and chili oil (if using) in a small bowl. Stir until the sugar is dissolved.
8. **Serve:** Serve the dumplings hot with the dipping sauce.

Cooking tips:
- If you like a crispy bottom on your dumplings, don't move them around in the pan once they've been placed. Let them cook undisturbed until the bottoms are golden brown.

NEW YEAR'S EVE

Dumplings are traditionally eaten during Chinese New Year celebrations as they symbolize wealth and good luck for the coming year.

Xiaolongbao

Xiaolongbao, often referred to as "soup dumplings" in English, are a type of steamed bun (baozi) from the Jiangnan region of China, especially associated with Shanghai and Wuxi.

They are traditionally prepared in small bamboo steaming baskets, which is where the name (literally meaning "little basket buns") comes from. Xiaolongbao are known for their delicate, thin skin and the rich, hot soup filling along with a meatball inside.

Eating xiaolongbao is a unique experience. You usually take a small bite to create an opening in the dumpling skin, then sip the soup out before eating the rest of the dumpling. It's a delicate balance of textures and flavors, with the savory soup, tender meat filling, and slightly chewy dumpling wrapper all coming together in one bite. This culinary delight makes xiaolongbao one of the most beloved dishes in Chinese cuisine.

6 SERVINGS   240 MINUTES   400 KCAL   EASY

INGREDIENTS

For the Dough:
- 2 cups all-purpose flour
- 3/4 cup water

For the Filling:
- 1/2 pound ground pork
- 1/4 cup finely chopped green onion
- 1/4 teaspoon white pepper
- 1/2 teaspoon salt
- 1 teaspoon soy sauce
- 1 teaspoon sesame oil

For the Gelatinized Broth:
- 2 cups chicken stock
- 1/2 packet of unflavored gelatin

For the Dipping Sauce:
- 1/4 cup soy sauce
- 1 tablespoon rice vinegar
- 1/2 teaspoon sugar
- 1 teaspoon finely shredded fresh ginger

DIRECTIONS

1. **Make the Gelatinized Broth:** Mix the chicken stock and gelatin in a pot and bring to a simmer until the gelatin is completely dissolved. Pour into a flat, shallow dish and refrigerate until set (about 2-3 hours).
2. **Make the Dough:** In a large mixing bowl, gradually add the water to the flour and knead into a smooth dough. This process should take about 10 minutes. Cover with a damp cloth and let the dough rest for an hour.
3. **Prepare the Filling:** In a large bowl, combine the ground pork, green onion, white pepper, salt, soy sauce, and sesame oil. Cut the set gelatinized broth into small cubes and add to the pork mixture. Mix well until the ingredients are thoroughly combined.
4. **Assemble the Dumplings:** Divide the rested dough into 24 equal pieces. Roll each piece into a small, thin, round disc about 4 inches in diameter.
5. Place a small spoonful of the filling in the center of each dough circle. Carefully pleat the dough to encase the filling and twist the top to seal. Repeat with the rest of the dough and filling.
6. **Cook the Dumplings:** Line a steamer basket with cabbage leaves or parchment paper. Place the dumplings in the basket, ensuring they do not touch each other. Steam over boiling water for about 8-10 minutes until the dumplings are translucent and cooked through.
7. **Make the Dipping Sauce:** Combine the soy sauce, vinegar, sugar, and shredded ginger in a small bowl. Stir until the sugar is dissolved.
8. **Serve:** Serve the dumplings hot with the dipping sauce. Carefully puncture the dumpling to let out steam before eating.

Cooking tips:
- Sealing the dumplings well is crucial to prevent the soup from leaking out during cooking.

Shengjianbao

Shengjianbao, also known as pan-fried soup dumplings, are a specialty of Shanghai, China. They are similar to xiaolongbao in terms of their juicy filling, but shengjianbao have a thicker, yeasted dough and are pan-fried to achieve a crispy bottom, resulting in a unique combination of texture and flavor.

Shengjianbao are traditionally filled with pork and gelatinized broth that melts into a flavorful soup during cooking. When you bite into a hot, freshly cooked shengjianbao, you'll get the taste of the tender pork filling and rich, savory soup, all wrapped in a soft and fluffy dough with a crispy bottom. The contrast between the soft top and crispy bottom, along with the soup explosion, make shengjianbao a beloved dish in Chinese cuisine.

4 SERVINGS   240 MINUTES   550 KCAL   MID

INGREDIENTS

For the Dough:
- 2 cups all-purpose flour
- 1/2 teaspoon yeast
- 1/2 cup warm water
- 1/2 teaspoon sugar
- A pinch of salt

For the Filling:
- 1/2 pound ground pork
- 1/4 cup finely chopped green onion
- 1/2 teaspoon white pepper
- 1 teaspoon sesame oil
- 1/2 teaspoon salt
- 1 teaspoon soy sauce

For the Gelatinized Broth:
- 2 cups chicken stock
- 1/2 packet of unflavored gelatin

For Cooking:
- 2 tablespoons vegetable oil
- 1/2 cup water
- 1 tablespoon sesame seeds

DIRECTIONS

1. **Make the Gelatinized Broth:** Mix the chicken stock and gelatin in a pot and bring to a simmer until the gelatin is completely dissolved. Pour into a flat, shallow dish and refrigerate until set (about 2-3 hours).
2. **Make the Dough:** Dissolve the yeast and sugar in the warm water and let sit for 5 minutes until frothy. In a large mixing bowl, combine the flour and salt. Gradually add the yeast water to the flour and knead into a smooth dough. This process should take about 10 minutes. Cover with a damp cloth and let the dough rise for 2 hours.
3. **Prepare the Filling:** In a large bowl, combine the ground pork, green onion, white pepper, salt, soy sauce, and sesame oil. Cut the set gelatinized broth into small cubes and add to the pork mixture. Mix well until the ingredients are thoroughly combined.
4. **Assemble the Dumplings:** Divide the risen dough into 24 equal pieces. Roll each piece into a small, thin, round disc about 4 inches in diameter.
5. Place a small spoonful of the filling in the center of each dough circle. Carefully pleat the dough to encase the filling and twist the top to seal. Repeat with the rest of the dough and filling.
6. **Cook the Dumplings:** Heat the vegetable oil in a large non-stick pan over medium-high heat. Place the dumplings in the pan, flat side down, and cook until the bottoms are golden brown, about 2-3 minutes. Sprinkle with sesame seeds.
7. Carefully pour the water into the pan and immediately cover with a lid. Cook for 10-12 minutes until the water evaporates and the dumplings are cooked through.
8. **Serve:** Serve the dumplings hot, ensuring they are cooled enough before eating to avoid burning your mouth with the hot soup inside.

Cooking tips:
- The gelatinized broth is what creates the "soup" inside the dumplings. Be sure to give it enough time to set before mixing it with the filling.

Har Gow

Har gow, also known as shrimp dumplings, are a staple of Cantonese dim sum. These translucent and shiny dumplings are loved for their thin, delicate wrapper and the generous filling of juicy, flavorful shrimp.

The dough for har gow is unique, made primarily from wheat and tapioca starch, and turns translucent when steamed. This allows you to see the pink shrimp filling inside, making it not only a delight to eat, but also to look at.

The art of making har gow lies in the balance of the thin yet sturdy wrapper that doesn't tear during cooking, and achieving the right texture and flavor in the shrimp filling. When done correctly, each bite of a har gow offers a slight chewiness from the wrapper, followed by the burst of savory, sweet shrimp filling. This iconic dim sum dish is a must-try for any lover of Chinese cuisine.

4 SERVINGS   120 MINUTES   250 KCAL   ☆ EASY

INGREDIENTS

For the Dough:
- 1 cup wheat starch
- 1/2 cup tapioca starch
- 1 cup boiling water
- 2 teaspoons vegetable oil

For the Filling:
- 1/2 pound shrimp, peeled and deveined
- 1 tablespoon finely chopped bamboo shoots
- 1/2 teaspoon salt
- 1/2 teaspoon sugar
- 1 teaspoon sesame oil
- 1/2 teaspoon white pepper
- 1 teaspoon cornstarch

DIRECTIONS

1. **Prepare the Dough:** In a large mixing bowl, combine the wheat starch and tapioca starch. Gradually pour in the boiling water while stirring. Add the oil and knead into a smooth dough. This process should take about 5 minutes. Cover with a damp cloth and let the dough rest for 30 minutes.
2. **Prepare the Filling:** Roughly chop the shrimp into small pieces. In a large bowl, combine the chopped shrimp, bamboo shoots, salt, sugar, sesame oil, white pepper, and cornstarch. Mix well until the ingredients are thoroughly combined.
3. **Assemble the Dumplings:** Divide the rested dough into 16 equal pieces. Roll each piece into a small, thin, round disc about 3 inches in diameter.
4. Place a small spoonful of the filling in the center of each dough circle. Fold the dough over the filling and pinch the edges to seal, creating pleats to form a half-moon shape. Repeat with the rest of the dough and filling.
5. **Cook the Dumplings:** Line a steamer basket with cabbage leaves or parchment paper. Place the dumplings in the basket, ensuring they do not touch each other. Steam over boiling water for about 6-8 minutes, until the dumplings are translucent and the shrimp are pink and cooked through.
6. **Serve:** Serve the dumplings hot with soy sauce or a chili sauce for dipping.

Cooking tips:
- The dough for har gow can be tricky to handle because it's quite sticky. Using a bit of oil on your hands can help.
- The pleating of har gow is an art form in itself. It may take some practice to get it right. If you struggle with it, simply sealing the dumplings without pleating is okay too.

MORE DIPS PLEASE

Dumplings are commonly enjoyed with dipping sauces such as soy sauce, vinegar, chili oil, or a combination of these flavors.

Siu Mai

Siu Mai, also known as shumai, is a type of traditional Chinese dumpling originating from Hohhot, Inner Mongolia. In Cantonese cuisine, Siu Mai is one of the most popular dim sum dishes. This type of dumpling is distinguished by its shape, which is a kind of open pouch.

These tasty dumplings are made by wrapping a thinly rolled piece of dough around a filling typically made of ground pork, chopped shrimp, and various seasonings. While the sides of the Siu Mai are pleated, the top is left open, providing a view of the filling inside.

Siu Mai has a juicy, flavorful filling and a slightly chewy wrapper. They are usually topped with an additional ingredient for garnish, like grated carrot, green pea, or even a small bit of roe, and are typically served with a side of soy sauce or chili sauce for dipping. A bite into one of these delicious dumplings allows you to experience a combination of savory meat, a slight crunch from the shrimp, and the soft, chewy dough.

 4 SERVINGS  90 MINUTES 300 KCAL EASY

INGREDIENTS

For the Filling:
- 1/2 pound ground pork
- 1/4 pound shrimp, peeled and deveined, finely chopped
- 1/4 cup finely chopped shiitake mushrooms
- 1 tablespoon soy sauce
- 1 tablespoon Shaoxing wine (or dry sherry)
- 1/2 teaspoon sesame oil
- 1/4 teaspoon white pepper
- 1 teaspoon sugar
- 1/2 teaspoon salt
- 2 teaspoons cornstarch
- 2 green onions, finely chopped

For the Wrappers and Topping:
- 24 wonton wrappers
- 1/4 cup finely grated carrot

DIRECTIONS

1. **Prepare the Filling:** In a large bowl, combine the ground pork, chopped shrimp, chopped mushrooms, soy sauce, Shaoxing wine, sesame oil, white pepper, sugar, salt, cornstarch, and green onions. Mix well until the ingredients are thoroughly combined.
2. **Assemble the Dumplings:** Place a wonton wrapper on a clean surface and spoon a heaped teaspoon of filling into the center. Gather the edges of the wrapper and fold up around the filling, pleating as you go and leaving the top of the filling exposed. Press down slightly to flatten the bottom so the dumpling can stand upright. Repeat with the rest of the wrappers and filling.
3. **Cook the Dumplings:** Line a steamer basket with cabbage leaves or parchment paper. Arrange the dumplings in the basket, ensuring they do not touch each other. Steam over boiling water for about 8-10 minutes, until the pork is cooked through.
4. **Serve:** Top each dumpling with a pinch of grated carrot for garnish. Serve the dumplings hot with soy sauce or a chili sauce for dipping.

Cooking tips:
- Siu Mai dumplings are traditionally open at the top, exposing the filling. This is unlike many other dumplings that are completely sealed. Make sure to leave the top of the filling exposed when you form the dumplings.
- You can also top the dumplings with a small piece of shrimp or a green pea for a different presentation.

FROZEN DUMPLINGS

Chinese dumplings can be frozen and stored for later consumption, making them a convenient and popular choice for quick meals.

Zongzi

Zongzi, also known as rice dumplings or sticky rice dumplings, is a traditional Chinese food made to celebrate the Dragon Boat Festival, which falls on the 5th day of the 5th month of the lunar calendar.

Zongzi is made of glutinous rice stuffed with different fillings, and wrapped in bamboo or reed leaves. They are usually cooked by steaming or boiling. The fillings used for zongzi vary from region to region, but the rice used is always sticky rice (also called glutinous rice).

In terms of taste, the sticky rice becomes tender and sticky after a long period of cooking, and it absorbs the flavors from the filling and the bamboo leaves. The result is a uniquely flavorful and aromatic food with a slight hint of a leafy fragrance, filled with ingredients that melt into the soft, sticky rice.

 6 SERVINGS   90 MINUTES 400 KCAL EASY

INGREDIENTS

For the Rice and Filling:
- 3 cups glutinous (sticky) rice
- 1/2 pound pork belly, cut into 1-inch pieces
- 1/4 cup soy sauce
- 1/4 cup Shaoxing wine (or dry sherry)
- 2 tablespoons brown sugar
- 1 teaspoon five-spice powder

Other Ingredients:
- 32 dried bamboo leaves
- Kitchen string
- 16 dried Chinese dates (optional)
- 16 chestnuts, pre-cooked and peeled (optional)

DIRECTIONS

1. **Soak the Rice and Bamboo Leaves:** Rinse the glutinous rice under cold water until the water runs clear. Place the rice in a large bowl, cover with water, and let soak for at least 6 hours or overnight. At the same time, soak the dried bamboo leaves in warm water overnight.
2. **Marinate the Pork:** In a large bowl, combine the pork belly pieces with the soy sauce, Shaoxing wine, brown sugar, and five-spice powder. Cover and refrigerate for at least 2 hours, or overnight.
3. **Prepare the Zongzi:** Drain the rice and the bamboo leaves. Lay two bamboo leaves flat on a clean surface, overlapping them lengthwise. Fold them up in the center to form a cone shape.
4. Spoon about 2 tablespoons of the soaked rice into the cone, then place a piece of marinated pork (and optionally a date and a chestnut) on top. Cover with another spoonful of rice. Fold the leaves over the top and wrap them tightly around the rice to form a pyramid shape. Secure the zongzi with kitchen string.
5. **Cook the Zongzi:** Place the wrapped zongzi in a large pot and add enough water to cover them completely. Bring the water to a boil, then reduce the heat to low, cover, and simmer for about 6 hours. If needed, check the water level occasionally and add more boiling water to keep the zongzi covered.
6. **Serve:** Allow the zongzi to cool slightly, then cut the strings and unwrap the leaves. Serve the zongzi warm.

Cooking tips:
- Wrapping zongzi takes practice. Don't be discouraged if your first few attempts are not perfect.
- You can add other ingredients to the filling, such as salted egg yolk, peanuts, or Chinese sausage.

Tangyuan

Tangyuan are sweet Chinese dumplings made from glutinous rice flour and typically filled with sweet black sesame paste. They are commonly served in a sweet soup and garnished with sweet Osmanthus flowers.

The dumplings are smooth and elastic, with a soft and chewy texture that contrasts beautifully with the rich, sweet, and slightly nutty black sesame filling. Tangyuan are traditionally eaten during the Lantern Festival, but are also enjoyed as a dessert or snack throughout the year.

Tangyuan have a special cultural significance in Chinese tradition. Their round shape symbolizes family unity and completeness, and the name tangyuan sounds similar to 'tuanyuan', which means 'reunion' in Chinese. Therefore, eating tangyuan is a way for Chinese people to express their longing for family members and their hopes for a happy and harmonious life.

4 SERVINGS   90 MINUTES   300 KCAL   EASY

INGREDIENTS

For the Dough:
- 2 cups glutinous (sticky) rice flour
- 3/4 cup warm water (you may need less or more)

For the Filling:
- 1/2 cup black sesame seeds
- 1/2 cup sugar
- 1/4 cup unsalted butter or lard

Other Ingredients:
- Water for boiling
- 1/2 cup sugar for sweet soup (optional)
- Sweet Osmanthus flowers for garnish (optional)

DIRECTIONS

1. **Prepare the Filling:** Toast the black sesame seeds in a dry pan over low heat until they are fragrant. Let them cool, then grind them in a food processor until they form a fine powder. Add the sugar and butter, and pulse until the ingredients come together in a paste. Refrigerate this filling for 1 hour.
2. **Prepare the Dough:** Put the rice flour in a mixing bowl. Gradually add warm water to the flour, stirring to mix. You want to create a smooth, pliable dough but not sticky. Add water slowly to make sure you don't make it too wet.
3. **Assemble the Tangyuan:** Pinch off a piece of dough (about 1 tablespoon) and flatten it in your hand. Place a small amount of the sesame filling in the center, then wrap the dough around it and roll it in your hands to form a ball. Make sure the filling is completely enclosed. Repeat with the rest of the dough and filling.
4. **Cook the Tangyuan:** Bring a large pot of water to a boil. Carefully drop the tangyuan into the boiling water. Cook them until they float to the surface, then continue to cook for another minute. If you're making a sweet soup, dissolve the additional sugar in a separate pot with a little water and add the cooked tangyuan to this sweet soup.
5. **Serve:** Use a slotted spoon to remove the tangyuan from the water or sweet soup and place them in serving bowls. If desired, garnish with sweet Osmanthus flowers. Serve hot.

Cooking tips:
- Make sure the filling is completely enclosed by the dough to prevent it from leaking out during boiling.
- You can also fill tangyuan with sweet red bean paste or even peanut butter.

Baozi

Baozi, or simply known as bao, are fluffy, steamed buns from Chinese cuisine that are often filled with a variety of ingredients. One of the most popular variants is filled with ground pork, seasoned with traditional Chinese sauces and spices.

Baozi have a slightly sweet, soft, and pillowy dough exterior that encases a savory, flavorful filling. The buns are steamed to perfection, resulting in a light and airy texture. When bitten into, the combination of the soft bun and the juicy filling provides a satisfying contrast.

Baozi are traditionally enjoyed for breakfast in China, but they can also be served as a main dish or a snack. They're a common sight in Chinese dim sum restaurants worldwide. These buns symbolize wealth and prosperity due to their round and plump appearance.

 4 SERVINGS 180 MINUTES  350 KCAL MID

INGREDIENTS

For the Dough:
- 4 cups all-purpose flour
- 1 cup warm water
- 2 tablespoons sugar
- 1 packet (about 2 1/4 teaspoons) active dry yeast
- 1 teaspoon baking powder

For the Filling:
- 1/2 pound ground pork
- 2 green onions, finely chopped
- 1 tablespoon soy sauce
- 1 tablespoon oyster sauce
- 1 tablespoon Shaoxing wine (or dry sherry)
- 1/2 teaspoon sesame oil
- 1/4 teaspoon white pepper
- 1/4 teaspoon sugar

DIRECTIONS

1. **Prepare the Dough:** Dissolve the sugar in the warm water and then stir in the yeast. Let it sit for 10 minutes, or until it's frothy. In a large bowl, combine the flour and baking powder. Gradually add the yeast mixture to the flour, kneading until a smooth, elastic dough forms. Cover the bowl with a damp cloth and let the dough rise in a warm place for about 2 hours, or until it doubles in size.
2. **Prepare the Filling:** In a large bowl, combine the ground pork, green onions, soy sauce, oyster sauce, Shaoxing wine, sesame oil, white pepper, and sugar. Mix until the ingredients are thoroughly combined.
3. **Assemble the Baozi:** After the dough has risen, punch it down and knead it for a few more minutes. Divide the dough into 12 equal pieces. Roll out each piece into a circle, keeping the center thicker than the edges. Spoon some of the pork filling into the center of the dough circle. Gather up the edges of the dough and pleat them together at the top to enclose the filling. Twist the top to seal it.
4. **Cook the Baozi:** Arrange the buns in a steamer, leaving some space between them to allow for expansion. Steam over high heat for about 15 minutes, then turn off the heat and let the buns sit for 5 minutes before removing the lid. This prevents the buns from collapsing.
5. **Serve:** Serve the baozi hot, as is or with soy sauce for dipping.

Cooking tips:
1. The dough should be smooth and not sticky. If it's too sticky, add a little more flour; if it's too dry, add a bit more water.
2. You can also fill baozi with other ingredients, such as vegetables, chicken, or sweet red bean paste.

DUMPLINGS LOTTERY

In some regions of China, there is a tradition of hiding a special treat, such as a coin or a sweet filling, inside one dumpling. The person who finds it is believed to receive good fortune or a special blessing.

Jian Dui

Jian Dui, also known as Sesame Seed Balls, are a popular sweet treat in Chinese cuisine. They are made of a glutinous rice dough filled with sweet red bean paste, rolled in sesame seeds, and then deep-fried until golden brown.

When fried, the Jian Dui puffs up, and the exterior becomes crisp and wonderfully sesame-flavored, while the interior remains soft and chewy with a sweet and smooth red bean filling. The contrasting textures and the combination of sweet and nutty flavors make them very enjoyable.

These sesame seed balls are often served during Chinese New Year and other festive occasions, symbolizing prosperity and the hope that your wealth will "expand" in the coming year, just like the balls expand when they're fried. However, they're also a common item in dim sum restaurants and are loved as a dessert or snack.

4 SERVINGS   90 MINUTES   200 KCAL   EASY

INGREDIENTS

For the Dough:
- 2 cups glutinous (sticky) rice flour
- 1/2 cup granulated sugar
- 3/4 cup warm water (you may need less or more)

For the Filling:
- 1/2 cup sweet red bean paste

Other Ingredients:
- 1 cup white sesame seeds
- Vegetable oil for frying

DIRECTIONS

1. **Prepare the Dough:** In a large bowl, combine the rice flour and sugar. Gradually add warm water, stirring until a dough forms. The dough should be soft but not sticky.
2. **Prepare the Balls**: Pinch off a small piece of dough (about 1 tablespoon) and flatten it into a disk. Place a small amount of red bean paste in the center of the disk, then wrap the dough around the filling and roll it into a ball. Make sure the filling is completely enclosed. Repeat with the remaining dough and filling.
3. **Coat the Balls:** Roll each ball in the sesame seeds until it's completely coated.
4. **Fry the Balls:** Heat the vegetable oil in a deep fryer or large, deep saucepan to 350°F (175°C). Fry the balls in batches, being careful not to overcrowd the pan. Cook until they're golden brown and have floated to the surface, about 3-4 minutes.
5. Serve: Use a slotted spoon to remove the balls from the oil and drain them on paper towels. Serve the Jian Dui warm.

Cooking tips:
- Make sure the filling is completely enclosed by the dough to prevent it from leaking out during frying.
- Don't make the balls too large, as they expand during frying.

DUMPINGS CONTESTS

Dumpling-making competitions are held in various parts of China, where participants showcase their skills in shaping and wrapping dumplings within a limited time frame.

Wontons

Wontons are a type of dumpling commonly found in a number of Chinese cuisines. They are usually made by spreading a square wonton wrapper, placing a small amount of filling in the center, and then molding the wonton into a desired shape by folding the wrapper and sealing its edges.

The fillings usually contain minced pork, shrimp, and various vegetables and seasonings, but the choices are very versatile. Wontons can be served in many ways, either deep-fried to a crispy golden brown or boiled and served in soup, often with noodles.

These delightful dumplings offer a delightful combination of textures, with a smooth and soft or crispy wrapper housing a savory, meaty filling. Whether enjoyed as a part of a main course, a side dish, or a snack, wontons bring comfort and satisfaction in every bite.

 4 SERVINGS    90 MINUTES   300 KCAL   EASY

INGREDIENTS

For the Filling:
- 1/2 pound ground pork
- 1/2 pound raw shrimp, peeled, deveined, and finely chopped
- 2 green onions, finely chopped
- 1 teaspoon soy sauce
- 1 teaspoon sesame oil
- 1/2 teaspoon ground white pepper
- 1/2 teaspoon grated fresh ginger
- 1/4 teaspoon salt

Other Ingredients:
- 40 wonton wrappers
- Water for sealing the wontons
- Vegetable oil for frying (optional)
- Water or broth for boiling (optional)

DIRECTIONS

1. **Prepare the Filling:** In a large bowl, combine the ground pork, chopped shrimp, green onions, soy sauce, sesame oil, white pepper, ginger, and salt. Mix well until all the ingredients are thoroughly combined.
2. **Assemble the Wontons:** Place a wonton wrapper on your work surface. Spoon a small amount of the pork and shrimp filling into the center of the wrapper. Dip your finger in water and moisten the edges of the wrapper. Fold the wrapper over the filling to form a triangle, pressing the edges to seal. If you like, you can fold the two opposite corners of the triangle over the filling and press them together to create a purse-like shape.
3. **Cook the Wontons**: At this point, you can choose to either deep-fry or boil your wontons. If frying, heat the vegetable oil in a deep fryer or large, deep saucepan to 350°F (175°C). Fry the wontons in batches until golden brown, then drain on paper towels. If boiling, bring a large pot of water or broth to a boil. Add the wontons, cooking until they float to the surface and the filling is cooked through.
4. **Serve:** Serve the wontons hot, as is or with soy sauce for dipping. If you boiled your wontons, you can also serve them in the cooking broth as a soup.

Cooking tips:
- Be careful not to overfill the wontons, or they may burst during cooking.
- Keep your wonton wrappers covered with a damp cloth while assembling them to prevent them from drying out.

Shuijiao

Shuijiao, which literally translates to "water dumplings," are a traditional Chinese dumpling typically filled with a mixture of ground meats and vegetables. They are called "water dumplings" because they are most commonly boiled (cooked in water), although they can also be steamed or pan-fried.

The dough for Shuijiao is made from simple wheat flour and water, creating a smooth and slightly chewy texture when cooked. The filling usually consists of ground pork and finely chopped vegetables such as Napa cabbage, green onions, and occasionally, mushrooms or chives. The dumplings are often served with a dipping sauce made from soy sauce and vinegar, and sometimes with a touch of chili oil for a bit of heat.

Shuijiao are a beloved dish in China, especially during the Lunar New Year and other special occasions. They symbolize wealth and prosperity due to their gold-like color and shape similar to ancient Chinese money. These dumplings are not only rich in flavor, but also in cultural significance.

4 SERVINGS　　120 MINUTES　　350 KCAL　　EASY

INGREDIENTS

For the Dough:
- 4 cups all-purpose flour
- 1 1/2 cups cold water

For the Filling:
- 1 pound ground pork
- 1 cup finely chopped Napa cabbage
- 3 green onions, finely chopped
- 2 cloves garlic, minced
- 1 tablespoon soy sauce
- 1 tablespoon sesame oil
- 1/2 teaspoon ground white pepper
- 1/2 teaspoon salt

Other Ingredients:
- Water for boiling the dumplings
- Soy sauce and vinegar for dipping (optional)

DIRECTIONS

1. **Prepare the Dough:** In a large bowl, combine the flour and water. Knead until a smooth, elastic dough forms. Cover the bowl with a damp cloth and let the dough rest for 30 minutes.
2. **Prepare the Filling:** In another large bowl, combine the ground pork, chopped Napa cabbage, green onions, minced garlic, soy sauce, sesame oil, white pepper, and salt. Mix until all the ingredients are thoroughly combined.
3. **Assemble the Dumplings:** Divide the dough into small pieces, about 1 inch in diameter. Roll out each piece into a thin circle. Place a spoonful of the pork and cabbage filling in the center of the dough circle. Fold the dough over the filling, pressing the edges together to seal and create a half-moon shape. You can also pleat the edges for a more traditional look.
4. **Cook the Dumplings:** Bring a large pot of water to a boil. Add the dumplings in batches, being careful not to overcrowd the pot. Cook until the dumplings float to the top and the dough becomes transparent, about 5-6 minutes.
5. **Serve:** Use a slotted spoon to remove the dumplings from the pot. If desired, serve the Shuijiao hot, with soy sauce and vinegar for dipping.

Cooking tips:
1. Be sure to finely chop the Napa cabbage and green onions so they mix well with the ground pork.
2. When sealing the dumplings, make sure there are no air pockets, as this could cause them to burst during cooking.

Hun Tun

Hun Tun, also known as Wonton Soup, is a comforting and popular dish in Chinese cuisine. It features small dumplings filled with a mixture of ground pork and finely chopped shrimp, which are then boiled in a flavorful broth made with chicken stock, ginger, and green onions.

The term "Hun Tun" is used in northern China, while "Wonton" is more commonly used in the south. Regardless of the name, these dumplings are celebrated for their delicate wrappers and savory fillings. When served in a hot soup, they create a warming, satisfying dish that's enjoyed as a staple in many Chinese households and restaurants.

The soup's simplicity allows the flavors of the wontons to shine through, while the ginger and green onions infuse the broth with a gentle, aromatic flavor. Whether enjoyed as a starter or a main course, Hun Tun is a delicious and nourishing dish that delights with every spoonful.

 4 SERVINGS 120 MINUTES  200 KCAL EASY

INGREDIENTS

For the Filling:
- 1/2 pound ground pork
- 1/2 pound raw shrimp, peeled, deveined, and finely chopped
- 3 green onions, finely chopped
- 1 teaspoon soy sauce
- 1 teaspoon sesame oil
- 1/2 teaspoon ground white pepper
- 1/2 teaspoon grated fresh ginger
- 1/4 teaspoon salt

Other Ingredients:
- 50 wonton wrappers
- Water for sealing the wontons

For the Soup:
- 8 cups chicken broth
- 1 inch piece of fresh ginger, peeled and thinly sliced
- 2 green onions, cut into 2-inch pieces
- Salt to taste

DIRECTIONS

1. **Prepare the Filling:** In a large bowl, combine the ground pork, chopped shrimp, green onions, soy sauce, sesame oil, white pepper, ginger, and salt. Mix well until all the ingredients are thoroughly combined.

2. **Assemble the Wontons:** Place a wonton wrapper on your work surface. Spoon a small amount of the pork and shrimp filling into the center of the wrapper. Dip your finger in water and moisten the edges of the wrapper. Fold the wrapper over the filling to form a triangle, pressing the edges to seal. You can then take the two longest points of the triangle and wrap them around to meet each other, forming a small ring shape with the filling securely in the center.

3. **Prepare the Soup:** In a large pot, combine the chicken broth, ginger, and green onions. Bring the broth to a boil, then reduce the heat and let it simmer for about 20 minutes. Strain the broth and discard the ginger and green onions. Season the broth with salt to taste.

4. **Cook the Wontons:** Return the broth to a boil. Add the wontons, cooking until they float to the surface and the filling is cooked through, about 5 minutes.

5. **Serve:** Ladle the soup and wontons into bowls. Serve the Hun Tun hot.

Cooking tips:
- Be careful not to overfill the wontons, or they may burst during cooking.
- Keep your wonton wrappers covered with a damp cloth while you're assembling the wontons to prevent them from drying out.

IT'S A RECORD!

The world's largest dumpling, as recognized by the Guinness World Records, weighed approximately 136 kilograms (300 pounds).

Fen Guo

Fen Guo is a type of Chinese dumpling made from glutinous rice flour, filled with a flavorful mixture of ground meat, mushrooms, and water chestnuts, then boiled until tender. The name "Fen Guo" literally translates to "rice dumpling" in English.

These dumplings are known for their tender, chewy skin made from glutinous rice flour, which has a slightly sweet flavor and a unique sticky texture. Inside, the filling is usually savory, made with a combination of finely minced meat, aromatic vegetables, and flavorful seasonings. The addition of water chestnuts and mushrooms adds a delightful crunch and umami flavor to the filling.

Once boiled, these dumplings become slightly transparent, revealing the enticing filling within. Fen Guo can be enjoyed as is, or served with a dipping sauce made from soy sauce and vinegar for added flavor. It's a versatile dish that can be enjoyed as a main course, a snack, or even a dessert if filled with sweet ingredients.

4 SERVINGS   120 MINUTES   300 KCAL   EASY

INGREDIENTS

For the Dough:
- 2 cups glutinous rice flour
- 1 cup water

For the Filling:
- 1/2 pound ground pork
- 1/2 cup finely chopped water chestnuts
- 3 shiitake mushrooms, soaked in warm water for 20 minutes, drained, and finely chopped
- 2 green onions, finely chopped
- 1 teaspoon soy sauce
- 1 teaspoon sesame oil
- 1/2 teaspoon ground white pepper
- 1/2 teaspoon salt

Other Ingredients:
- Water for boiling the dumplings
- Soy sauce and vinegar for dipping (optional)

DIRECTIONS

1. **Prepare the Dough:** In a large bowl, combine the glutinous rice flour and water. Knead until a smooth, pliable dough forms. Cover the bowl with a damp cloth and let the dough rest for 30 minutes.
2. **Prepare the Filling:** In another large bowl, combine the ground pork, chopped water chestnuts, chopped shiitake mushrooms, green onions, soy sauce, sesame oil, white pepper, and salt. Mix until all the ingredients are thoroughly combined.
3. **Assemble the Dumplings:** Divide the dough into small pieces, about 1 inch in diameter. Flatten each piece into a thin circle. Place a spoonful of the pork and water chestnut filling in the center of the dough circle. Fold the dough over the filling, pressing the edges together to seal and create a half-moon shape.
4. **Cook the Dumplings:** Bring a large pot of water to a boil. Add the dumplings in batches, being careful not to overcrowd the pot. Cook until the dumplings float to the top and the filling is cooked through, about 5-6 minutes.
5. **Serve:** Use a slotted spoon to remove the dumplings from the pot. Serve the Fen Guo hot, with soy sauce and vinegar for dipping, if desired.

Cooking tips:
- Be sure to finely chop the water chestnuts and shiitake mushrooms so they mix well with the ground pork.
- When sealing the dumplings, make sure there are no air pockets, as this could cause them to burst during cooking.

Chao Shou

Chao Shou is a spicy variation of Chinese wontons originating from the Sichuan province. The name "Chao Shou" translates to "folded hands," referring to the unique way these dumplings are folded to resemble a person folding their hands.

Unlike the clear soup-based wontons commonly found in other Chinese cuisines, Chao Shou is served with a spicy and aromatic chili oil, bringing out the rich flavors of Sichuan cuisine, known for its bold and pungent flavors.

The filling is typically made from ground pork, Napa cabbage, and seasonings. Once the wontons are assembled, they are boiled in a flavorful broth until cooked. To finish, the cooked Chao Shou are drizzled with homemade chili oil, creating a satisfyingly spicy and savory dish with a bit of a kick. These Sichuan wontons offer a delightful experience of textures and flavors that are sure to leave a lasting impression.

🍴 4 SERVINGS   🕐 90 MINUTES   🔥 400 KCAL   ☆ MID

INGREDIENTS

For the Filling:
- 1/2 pound ground pork
- 1/2 cup finely chopped Napa cabbage
- 2 green onions, finely chopped
- 1 tablespoon soy sauce
- 1 teaspoon sesame oil
- 1/2 teaspoon ground white pepper
- 1/2 teaspoon grated fresh ginger
- 1/4 teaspoon salt

Other Ingredients:
- 50 wonton wrappers
- Water for sealing the wontons
- 4 cups of chicken broth for cooking the wontons

For the Chili Oil:
- 1/4 cup sesame oil
- 2 tablespoons Sichuan chili flakes (adjust to taste)
- 1 teaspoon Chinese five-spice powder

DIRECTIONS

1. **Prepare the Filling:** In a large bowl, combine the ground pork, chopped Napa cabbage, green onions, soy sauce, sesame oil, white pepper, ginger, and salt. Mix well until all the ingredients are thoroughly combined.

2. **Assemble the Wontons:** Place a wonton wrapper on your work surface. Spoon a small amount of the pork filling into the center of the wrapper. Dip your finger in water and moisten the edges of the wrapper. Fold the wrapper over the filling to form a triangle, pressing the edges to seal. You can then take the two longest points of the triangle and wrap them around to meet each other, forming a small ring shape with the filling securely in the center.

3. **Prepare the Chili Oil:** Heat the sesame oil in a small saucepan over medium heat until it is warm but not smoking. Remove from heat and stir in the Sichuan chili flakes and five-spice powder. Let the mixture steep for at least 30 minutes.

4. **Cook the Wontons:** In a large pot, bring the chicken broth to a boil. Add the wontons and cook until they float to the top and the filling is cooked through, about 5 minutes.

5. **Serve:** Use a slotted spoon to remove the wontons from the pot. Drizzle the chili oil over the wontons before serving. Serve the Chao Shou hot.

Cooking tips:
- Make sure your chili oil is not too hot when you add the chili flakes and five-spice powder, or the spices may burn.
- Keep your wonton wrappers covered with a damp cloth while you're assembling the wontons to prevent them from drying out.

Shumai

Shumai, also known as siu mai, is a type of traditional Chinese dumpling originating from Hohhot, Inner Mongolia. These dumplings are easily recognizable by their unique open-faced design, which allows you to see the juicy filling within.

The filling is usually a savory blend of ground pork, shiitake mushrooms, water chestnuts, and a variety of seasonings. Unlike many other types of dumplings, shumai are not sealed at the top, allowing the beautiful filling to be displayed.

Shumai are usually cooked by steaming, which keeps the wrapper soft and the filling juicy. They are typically served with soy sauce for dipping and can be garnished with peas or finely diced carrots for added color and texture.

These dumplings are a staple in dim sum cuisine and are enjoyed for their delicate, pleated wrapper and flavorful filling. Whether they're served as part of a larger meal or enjoyed on their own as a light snack, shumai offer a delightful mix of textures and flavors that are sure to please.

 4 SERVINGS  90 MINUTES 400 KCAL EASY

INGREDIENTS

For the Filling:
- 1/2 pound ground pork
- 1/4 cup finely chopped shiitake mushrooms
- 1/4 cup finely chopped water chestnuts
- 2 green onions, finely chopped
- 1 tablespoon soy sauce
- 1 tablespoon Shaoxing wine
- 1 teaspoon sesame oil
- 1/2 teaspoon sugar
- 1/4 teaspoon ground white pepper
- 1/4 teaspoon salt

Other Ingredients:
- 24 wonton wrappers
- Peas or finely diced carrots for garnish (optional)
- Soy sauce for serving

DIRECTIONS

1. **Prepare the Filling:** In a large bowl, combine the ground pork, chopped shiitake mushrooms, chopped water chestnuts, green onions, soy sauce, Shaoxing wine, sesame oil, sugar, white pepper, and salt. Mix well until all the ingredients are thoroughly combined.
2. **Assemble the Dumplings:** Place a wonton wrapper on your work surface. Spoon a small amount of the pork filling into the center of the wrapper. Gather the edges of the wrapper and pleat them around the filling, leaving the top of the filling exposed. If desired, top each dumpling with a pea or small piece of carrot for garnish.
3. **Cook the Dumplings:** Arrange the assembled dumplings in a bamboo steamer, making sure they don't touch each other. Steam over high heat for about 15 minutes, or until the filling is cooked through.
4. **Serve:** Serve the Shumai hot, with soy sauce for dipping.

Cooking tips:
- Be careful not to overfill your dumplings, or they may burst during cooking.
- When arranging the dumplings in the steamer, make sure there is enough space between each one to prevent them from sticking together.

Fried Wontons

Fried wontons are a popular appetizer in Chinese cuisine, known for their crispy texture and savory filling. These bite-sized treats consist of a thin wonton wrapper filled with a flavorful mixture of ground pork, shrimp, and various seasonings.

Once the wontons are assembled, they are quickly fried to a golden brown, resulting in a crispy outer shell and a juicy, flavorful interior. The wontons can be served plain or with a side of sweet and sour sauce, which adds a tangy contrast to the savory filling.

Whether enjoyed as a snack, appetizer, or part of a larger meal, fried wontons are a delightful blend of textures and flavors. Their satisfying crunch and flavorful filling make them a favorite among both children and adults.

 6 SERVINGS   90 MINUTES    400 KCAL   MID

INGREDIENTS

For the Filling:
- 1/2 pound ground pork
- 1/2 cup finely chopped shrimp
- 1/4 cup finely chopped water chestnuts
- 1 green onion, finely chopped
- 1 teaspoon soy sauce
- 1 teaspoon Shaoxing wine
- 1/2 teaspoon sesame oil
- 1/2 teaspoon sugar
- 1/4 teaspoon ground white pepper
- 1/4 teaspoon salt

Other Ingredients:
- 40 wonton wrappers
- Water for sealing the wontons
- Vegetable oil for frying
- Sweet and sour sauce for serving

DIRECTIONS

1. **Prepare the Filling:** In a large bowl, combine the ground pork, chopped shrimp, chopped water chestnuts, green onion, soy sauce, Shaoxing wine, sesame oil, sugar, white pepper, and salt. Mix well until all the ingredients are thoroughly combined.
2. **Assemble the Wontons:** Place a wonton wrapper on your work surface. Spoon a small amount of the pork and shrimp filling into the center of the wrapper. Dip your finger in water and moisten the edges of the wrapper. Fold the wrapper over the filling to form a triangle, pressing the edges to seal.
3. **Fry the Wontons:** Heat about 2 inches of vegetable oil in a deep fryer or large, heavy pot to 375°F (190°C). Fry the wontons in batches until golden brown, about 2-3 minutes, turning occasionally. Use a slotted spoon to transfer the fried wontons to paper towels to drain.
4. **Serve:** Serve the Fried Wontons hot, with sweet and sour sauce for dipping.

Cooking tips:
1. Be sure not to overcrowd the pot when frying the wontons, as this can lower the oil's temperature and result in soggy wontons.
2. For a lighter version, the wontons can also be steamed or boiled instead of fried.

Momo

Momo is a type of South Asian dumpling that is popular in Tibet, Nepal, Bhutan, and parts of India. It is made with a simple dough and filled with a variety of ingredients, though ground meat (commonly pork or beef) and vegetables are typical.

The momos are usually shaped into a round, pleated design and then steamed until the dough becomes firm and the filling is cooked. This results in a dumpling that is soft and slightly chewy on the outside, with a juicy, flavorful filling on the inside.

Momos are often served with a dipping sauce, such as soy sauce or a spicy chutney, which enhances the flavors of the dumpling. Whether enjoyed as a snack, a main dish, or part of a larger meal, momos are a comforting and delicious food that offers a taste of Himalayan cuisine.

 4 SERVINGS   120 MINUTES   300 KCAL   EASY

INGREDIENTS

For the Dough:
- 2 cups all-purpose flour
- About 3/4 cup water (adjust as needed)
- 1/2 teaspoon salt

For the Filling:
- 1/2 pound ground pork or beef
- 1/2 cup finely chopped cabbage
- 1/2 cup finely chopped onion
- 2 cloves garlic, minced
- 1 tablespoon soy sauce
- 1/2 teaspoon ground black pepper
- 1/2 teaspoon salt

Other Ingredients:
- Soy sauce or hot sauce for serving

DIRECTIONS

1. **Prepare the Dough:** In a large bowl, combine the flour and salt. Gradually add water, kneading until a smooth dough forms. Cover the dough and let it rest for about 30 minutes.
2. **Prepare the Filling:** In a large bowl, combine the ground meat, chopped cabbage, chopped onion, minced garlic, soy sauce, black pepper, and salt. Mix well until all the ingredients are thoroughly combined.
3. **Assemble the Dumplings:** Divide the dough into small balls, about 1 inch in diameter. On a floured surface, roll out each ball into a thin circle. Place a small amount of filling in the center of each circle. Fold the dough over the filling and pinch the edges together to seal, creating a pleated pattern.
4. **Cook the Dumplings:** Arrange the dumplings in a steamer, ensuring they don't touch each other. Steam over high heat for about 15 minutes, or until the filling is cooked through and the dough is firm.
5. **Serve:** Serve the Momos hot, with soy sauce or hot sauce for dipping.

Cooking tips:
- Be sure not to overfill the dumplings, as they may burst during cooking.
- Keep the assembled dumplings covered with a damp cloth until you're ready to cook them to prevent them from drying out.

"POTSTICKERS"

Chinese dumplings are often boiled or steamed, but they can also be pan-fried, creating a crispy texture known as "potstickers."

Crystal Dumplings

Crystal dumplings, also known as Har Gow in Cantonese, are a type of Chinese dumpling that are a staple in dim sum cuisine. They are named for their beautiful, translucent wrappers, which are made from a combination of wheat and tapioca starch. The dough becomes transparent when steamed, revealing the colorful filling inside.

The filling for crystal dumplings often includes ingredients like shrimp, bamboo shoots, and green onions, creating a flavorful mix that contrasts beautifully with the delicate, slightly chewy wrapper.

Crystal dumplings are usually steamed until the dough becomes translucent and the filling is cooked through, resulting in a dumpling that is as delicious to eat as it is beautiful to look at. They are typically served with a side of soy sauce or chili sauce for dipping.

4 SERVINGS   90 MINUTES   200 KCAL   EASY

INGREDIENTS

For the Dough:

- 1 cup wheat starch
- 1/2 cup tapioca starch
- 1/4 teaspoon salt
- 1 cup boiling water
- 1 tablespoon vegetable oil

For the Filling:

- 1/2 pound raw shrimp, peeled, deveined, and chopped
- 1/2 cup finely chopped bamboo shoots
- 1 green onion, finely chopped
- 1 tablespoon oyster sauce
- 1 teaspoon sesame oil
- 1/4 teaspoon ground white pepper
- 1/4 teaspoon salt

Other Ingredients:

- Soy sauce or chili sauce for serving

DIRECTIONS

1. **Prepare the Dough:** In a large bowl, combine the wheat starch, tapioca starch, and salt. Gradually pour in the boiling water while stirring. Add the vegetable oil and knead until a smooth dough forms. Cover and set aside to rest.
2. **Prepare the Filling:** In a separate bowl, combine the chopped shrimp, bamboo shoots, green onion, oyster sauce, sesame oil, white pepper, and salt. Mix well until all the ingredients are thoroughly combined.
3. **Assemble the Dumplings:** Divide the dough into small pieces and roll each one into a ball. Flatten each ball into a thin disc. Place a spoonful of the shrimp filling in the center of each disc. Fold the dough over the filling and pinch the edges together to seal, creating a half-moon shape.
4. **Cook the Dumplings:** Arrange the dumplings in a bamboo steamer, making sure they don't touch each other. Steam over high heat for about 15 minutes, or until the dough becomes translucent and the filling is cooked through.
5. **Serve:** Serve the Crystal Dumplings hot, with soy sauce or chili sauce for dipping.

Cooking tips:

1. The dough for crystal dumplings can be a bit tricky to work with as it's stickier than regular dumpling dough. Dust your hands with some tapioca starch to prevent sticking.
2. Be sure not to overfill the dumplings, as they may burst during cooking.

Gyoza

Gyoza are Japanese dumplings that are similar to Chinese jiaozi. They consist of a thin wrapper filled with a flavorful mix of ground pork, cabbage, and various seasonings. The filled wrappers are then folded into a pleated crescent shape, which is a characteristic feature of gyoza.

The cooking method for gyoza is what sets them apart. They are first pan-fried until the bottoms become crispy, and then water is added and the pan is covered to steam and cook the rest of the dumpling. This results in a dumpling with a unique texture that is crispy on the bottom and tender on the top.

Gyoza are typically served with a dipping sauce made of soy sauce and rice vinegar, and sometimes a bit of chili oil. Whether enjoyed as a snack, appetizer, or part of a larger meal, gyoza are a delicious and satisfying dish that offers a taste of Japanese cuisine.

 4 SERVINGS   90 MINUTES    300 KCAL   EASY

INGREDIENTS

For the Filling:

- 1/2 pound ground pork
- 2 cups finely chopped cabbage
- 2 green onions, finely chopped
- 1 clove garlic, minced
- 1 teaspoon grated ginger
- 1 tablespoon soy sauce
- 1 teaspoon sesame oil
- 1/4 teaspoon salt
- 1/4 teaspoon ground black pepper

Other Ingredients:

- 40 gyoza wrappers
- 2 tablespoons vegetable oil
- 1/2 cup water
- Soy sauce, for serving
- Rice vinegar, for serving

DIRECTIONS

1. **Prepare the Filling:** In a large bowl, combine the ground pork, chopped cabbage, green onions, garlic, ginger, soy sauce, sesame oil, salt, and pepper. Mix well until all the ingredients are thoroughly combined.
2. **Assemble the Gyoza:** Place a gyoza wrapper on your work surface. Spoon a small amount of the pork and cabbage filling onto the center of the wrapper. Moisten the edges of the wrapper with water, fold it in half over the filling, and pinch the edges to seal. Repeat with the remaining wrappers and filling.
3. **Cook the Gyoza**: Heat the vegetable oil in a large non-stick skillet over medium-high heat. Arrange the gyoza in the skillet, flat side down, and cook until the bottoms are golden brown, about 2-3 minutes. Pour in the water, cover the skillet, and reduce the heat to medium. Let the gyoza steam until the water has evaporated and the bottoms are crispy and golden, about 10 minutes.
4. **Serve:** Serve the Gyoza hot, with soy sauce and rice vinegar for dipping.

Cooking tips:

1. Be careful not to overcrowd the pan when cooking the gyoza. They should not touch each other, or they may stick together.
2. The amount of water added to the skillet can be adjusted depending on how crispy you prefer the gyoza.

"INGOTS"

The shape of Chinese dumplings, usually resembling a crescent or half-moon, is said to have been inspired by ancient Chinese currency called ingots.

Cha Guo

Cha Guo, or Taro Cake, is a traditional Chinese dish often served during the Lunar New Year, but it is also popular as a snack or appetizer in dim sum. The main ingredient is taro, a starchy root vegetable that is grated and mixed with other ingredients like Chinese sausage, dried shrimp, and green onions. This mixture is then combined with a batter made from rice flour and water, poured into a cake pan, and steamed until it sets.

The result is a savory cake with a unique, slightly chewy texture and rich, umami flavor. The taro gives the cake a slightly sweet, nutty flavor that pairs well with the salty Chinese sausage and dried shrimp. Cha Guo can be served hot or at room temperature, and it's usually garnished with chopped green onions for added flavor and color.

 4 SERVINGS   120 MINUTES   250 KCAL   EASY

INGREDIENTS

- 2 cups grated taro
- 1 cup rice flour
- 2 cups water
- 2 Chinese sausages, diced
- 1/2 cup dried shrimp, soaked and chopped
- 2 green onions, chopped
- 1 tablespoon vegetable oil
- 1/2 teaspoon salt
- 1/2 teaspoon white pepper

DIRECTIONS

1. **Prepare the Ingredients:** Rinse the dried shrimp under cold water, then soak them in hot water for about 15 minutes. Once they're soft, chop them into small pieces.
2. **Cook the Ingredients:** Heat the oil in a large pan over medium heat. Add the Chinese sausages and cook until they start to turn brown. Then, add the chopped shrimp and cook for a few more minutes until they're fragrant.
3. **Combine the Ingredients:** Add the grated taro to the pan and mix everything together. Cook for a few more minutes, then remove the pan from heat.
4. **Prepare the Batter:** In a separate bowl, mix the rice flour, water, salt, and white pepper together until there are no lumps. Pour this batter over the cooked ingredients in the pan and mix well.
5. **Cook the Cha Guo:** Pour the mixture into a greased 9-inch round cake pan. Steam over high heat for 45 minutes, or until the taro cake sets.
6. **Serve:** Allow the taro cake to cool, then cut it into pieces. Garnish with chopped green onions and serve.

Cooking tips

- Make sure to soak the dried shrimp until they're soft enough to chop. If they're still hard, they may not cook properly.
- Steam the taro cake until it sets and becomes translucent. If it's still opaque, it may need more time.

Peking Ravioli

Peking Ravioli, also known as potstickers or guotie, are a type of Chinese dumpling that are popular in both China and the United States. They were famously renamed "Peking Ravioli" in the Boston area by Joyce Chen, a well-known restaurateur and chef, as a way to make the dish more familiar and appealing to American customers.

Peking Ravioli are made by filling a thin dough wrapper with a mixture of ground pork, cabbage, and other seasonings. The dumplings are then pan-fried on one side to create a crispy, golden crust, and steamed on the other side to keep the inside tender and juicy. This unique combination of textures, along with the savory, umami flavor of the filling, makes Peking Ravioli a delicious and satisfying dish that can be enjoyed as an appetizer, snack, or main course.

4 SERVINGS   90 MINUTES   350 KCAL   EASY

INGREDIENTS

For the Filling:
- 1/2 pound ground pork
- 1/2 cup finely chopped Napa cabbage
- 2 green onions, finely chopped
- 1 clove garlic, minced
- 1 teaspoon grated ginger
- 1 tablespoon soy sauce
- 1 teaspoon sesame oil
- 1/4 teaspoon salt
- 1/4 teaspoon ground black pepper

Other Ingredients:
- 40 dumpling wrappers
- 2 tablespoons vegetable oil
- 1/2 cup water
- Soy sauce, for serving
- Rice vinegar, for serving

DIRECTIONS

1. **Prepare the Filling:** In a large bowl, combine the ground pork, chopped cabbage, green onions, garlic, ginger, soy sauce, sesame oil, salt, and pepper. Mix well until all the ingredients are thoroughly combined.
2. **Assemble the Dumplings:** Place a dumpling wrapper on your work surface. Spoon a small amount of the pork and cabbage filling onto the center of the wrapper. Moisten the edges of the wrapper with water, fold it in half over the filling, and pinch the edges to seal. Repeat with the remaining wrappers and filling.
3. **Cook the Dumplings:** Heat the vegetable oil in a large non-stick skillet over medium-high heat. Arrange the dumplings in the skillet, flat side down, and cook until the bottoms are golden brown, about 2-3 minutes. Pour in the water, cover the skillet, and reduce the heat to medium. Let the dumplings steam until the water has evaporated and the bottoms are crispy and golden, about 10 minutes.
4. **Serve:** Serve the Peking Ravioli hot, with soy sauce and rice vinegar for dipping.

Cooking tips:
- Be careful not to overcrowd the pan when cooking the dumplings. They should not touch each other, or they may stick together.
- The amount of water added to the skillet can be adjusted depending on how crispy you prefer the dumplings.

Ham Sui Gok

Ham Sui Gok, or Cantonese fried dumplings, are a popular dish in dim sum. They feature a savory filling of ground pork and diced bamboo shoots, encased in a sweet, glutinous dough. This dough is made from a mixture of wheat and tapioca starch, which gives the dumplings their distinctive chewy texture and golden color when fried.

The contrast between the sweet, crispy exterior and the savory, juicy interior is what makes Ham Sui Gok so delicious and unique. Despite their complexity, these dumplings are well worth the effort and are sure to be a hit at any gathering.

4 SERVINGS   90 MINUTES   450 KCAL   MID

INGREDIENTS

For the Filling:
- 1/2 pound ground pork
- 1/2 cup diced bamboo shoots
- 2 green onions, finely chopped
- 1 clove garlic, minced
- 1 teaspoon soy sauce
- 1 teaspoon oyster sauce
- 1/2 teaspoon sugar
- 1/2 teaspoon cornstarch
- 1/4 teaspoon ground black pepper

For the Dough:
- 1 cup wheat starch
- 1/2 cup tapioca starch
- 1/2 cup sugar
- 1 cup boiling water
- 2 tablespoons vegetable oil
- For Frying:
- Vegetable oil

DIRECTIONS

1. **Prepare the Filling:** In a large bowl, combine the ground pork, bamboo shoots, green onions, garlic, soy sauce, oyster sauce, sugar, cornstarch, and pepper. Mix well until all the ingredients are thoroughly combined.
2. **Prepare the Dough:** In a separate bowl, combine the wheat starch, tapioca starch, and sugar. Add the boiling water and oil, and mix until a dough forms.
3. **Assemble the Dumplings:** Take a small piece of dough and flatten it into a round disc. Place a spoonful of the pork filling in the center, then fold the dough over the filling and pinch the edges to seal. Repeat with the remaining dough and filling.
4. **Fry the Dumplings:** Heat about 2 inches of vegetable oil in a deep pot over medium-high heat. Fry the dumplings in batches until golden brown, about 5-7 minutes. Drain on paper towels.
5. **Serve:** Serve the Ham Sui Gok hot. They are typically enjoyed on their own, or with a side of soy sauce for dipping.

Cooking tips:

1. Make sure the oil is hot enough before you start frying. You can test this by dropping a small piece of dough into the oil. If it sizzles and floats to the top, the oil is ready.
2. Be careful not to overcrowd the pot when frying the dumplings. They should not touch each other, or they may stick together.

BREAKFAST ANYONE?

In Northern China, dumplings are traditionally served during breakfast or brunch and are commonly accompanied by a bowl of hot soup.

Pork and Peanut Dumplings

Pork and Peanut Dumplings are a delicious variation on traditional Chinese dumplings, featuring a savory filling that includes ground pork and finely chopped peanuts for added texture and flavor. The filling is also made with Napa cabbage, green onions, and various seasonings, which complement the rich, nutty flavor of the peanuts and the umami flavor of the pork.

The dumplings are assembled by placing a spoonful of filling onto a thin dough wrapper, which is then folded in half and the edges are pinched to seal. The dumplings are pan-fried on one side to create a crispy, golden crust, and then steamed on the other side to keep the inside tender and juicy. This unique combination of textures and flavors makes Pork and Peanut Dumplings a favorite among both dumpling connoisseurs and novices alike.

 4 SERVINGS  90 MINUTES 400 KCAL MID

INGREDIENTS

For the Filling:
- 1/2 pound ground pork
- 1/4 cup finely chopped peanuts
- 1/2 cup finely chopped Napa cabbage
- 2 green onions, finely chopped
- 1 clove garlic, minced
- 1 teaspoon grated ginger
- 1 tablespoon soy sauce
- 1 teaspoon sesame oil
- 1/4 teaspoon salt
- 1/4 teaspoon ground black pepper

Other Ingredients:
- 40 dumpling wrappers
- 2 tablespoons vegetable oil
- 1/2 cup water
- Soy sauce, for serving
- Rice vinegar, for serving

DIRECTIONS

1. **Prepare the Filling:** In a large bowl, combine the ground pork, chopped peanuts, cabbage, green onions, garlic, ginger, soy sauce, sesame oil, salt, and pepper. Mix well until all the ingredients are thoroughly combined.
2. **Assemble the Dumplings:** Place a dumpling wrapper on your work surface. Spoon a small amount of the pork and peanut filling onto the center of the wrapper. Moisten the edges of the wrapper with water, fold it in half over the filling, and pinch the edges to seal. Repeat with the remaining wrappers and filling.
3. **Cook the Dumplings**: Heat the vegetable oil in a large non-stick skillet over medium-high heat. Arrange the dumplings in the skillet, flat side down, and cook until the bottoms are golden brown, about 2-3 minutes. Pour in the water, cover the skillet, and reduce the heat to medium. Let the dumplings steam until the water has evaporated and the bottoms are crispy and golden, about 10 minutes.
4. **Serve:** Serve the Pork and Peanut Dumplings hot, with soy sauce and rice vinegar for dipping.

Cooking tips:
1. Be careful not to overcrowd the pan when cooking the dumplings. They should not touch each other, or they may stick together.
2. The amount of water added to the skillet can be adjusted depending on how crispy you prefer the dumplings.

Lamb and Coriander Dumplings

Lamb and Coriander Dumplings are a flavorful variation of traditional Chinese dumplings. The filling is made with ground lamb, which is flavorful and tender, along with fresh coriander (also known as cilantro) that lends a distinct, refreshing taste. This combination of lamb and coriander is a classic pairing in many cuisines due to their complementary flavors.

The dumplings are assembled by placing a spoonful of filling onto a thin dough wrapper, which is then folded in half and the edges are pinched to seal. The dumplings are pan-fried on one side to create a crispy, golden crust, and then steamed on the other side to keep the inside tender and juicy. Lamb and Coriander Dumplings are truly a treat for the palate, offering a balance of robust and fresh flavors.

 4 SERVINGS    90 MINUTES   400 KCAL   EASY

INGREDIENTS

For the Filling:
- 1/2 pound ground lamb
- 1/2 cup fresh coriander (cilantro), finely chopped
- 2 green onions, finely chopped
- 1 clove garlic, minced
- 1 teaspoon grated ginger
- 1 tablespoon soy sauce
- 1 teaspoon sesame oil
- 1/4 teaspoon salt
- 1/4 teaspoon ground black pepper

Other Ingredients:
- 40 dumpling wrappers
- 2 tablespoons vegetable oil
- 1/2 cup water
- Soy sauce, for serving
- Rice vinegar, for serving

DIRECTIONS

1. **Prepare the Filling:** In a large bowl, combine the ground lamb, chopped coriander, green onions, garlic, ginger, soy sauce, sesame oil, salt, and pepper. Mix well until all the ingredients are thoroughly combined.
2. **Assemble the Dumplings:** Place a dumpling wrapper on your work surface. Spoon a small amount of the lamb and coriander filling onto the center of the wrapper. Moisten the edges of the wrapper with water, fold it in half over the filling, and pinch the edges to seal. Repeat with the remaining wrappers and filling.
3. **Cook the Dumplings:** Heat the vegetable oil in a large non-stick skillet over medium-high heat. Arrange the dumplings in the skillet, flat side down, and cook until the bottoms are golden brown, about 2-3 minutes. Pour in the water, cover the skillet, and reduce the heat to medium. Let the dumplings steam until the water has evaporated and the bottoms are crispy and golden, about 10 minutes.
4. **Serve:** Serve the Lamb and Coriander Dumplings hot, with soy sauce and rice vinegar for dipping.

Cooking tips:
- Be careful not to overcrowd the pan when cooking the dumplings. They should not touch each other, or they may stick together.
- The amount of water added to the skillet can be adjusted depending on how crispy you prefer the dumplings.

Made in the USA
Las Vegas, NV
24 January 2024

84828741R00036